W

A Way of the Cross
for Eucharistic Adoration

Portia Webster

Liguori
ONE LIGUORI DRIVE
LIGUORI MO 63057-9999

To Reverend Father Bruno Barnhart, O.S.B. Cam.

~

Imprimi Potest:
Thomas D. Picton, C.Ss.R.
Provincial, Denver Province
The Redemptorists

Imprimatur: Most Reverend Robert J. Hermann,
Auxiliary Bishop, Archdiocese of St. Louis

ISBN 0-7648-1436-2
© 2006, Liguori Publications
Printed in the United States of America
10 09 08 07 06 5 4 3 2

Scripture quotations are from the *New Revised Standard
Version of the Bible*, © 1989 by the Division of Christian
Education of the National Council of Churches of Christ
in the USA. Used with permission. All rights reserved.

Interior Art: Andy Willham

Liguori Publications, a nonprofit corporation, is an
apostolate of the Redemptorists. To learn more about the
Redemptorists, visit Redemptorists.com.

To order, call 1-800-325-9521
www.liguori.org

Introduction

IN FALL 1994, I made the Ignatian exercises at the Spiritual Ministry Center in San Diego, California. One of the assignments was to meditate on stations two, four, and seven of the Way of the Cross. I did the assignment, but only in holy Communion did I deeply experience the journey our Lord made for our salvation. At the urging of spiritual directors, I completed the rest of the stations over the years.

We Adore Thee is not a typical Way of the Cross; it is a personal, intimate dialogue of the soul with Jesus and is best suited for individual use. It can be prayed entirely in one sitting, but you might find it most fruitful if you use only one section at a time. Writing this Way of the Cross has been a grace-filled journey for me, and it is my hope and prayer that reading it will be one for you.

My thanks to the priests, sisters, mentors, and friends who have read this manuscript through the years and urged me to have it published. For the past ten years I have had the privilege of living in silence and solitude on the grounds of an Olivetan Benedictine Monastery in Arizona. My thanks to almighty God, who has made all of these graces possible.

Jesus Is Condemned to Death on the Cross

*"Be merciful,
just as your Father
is merciful."*

LUKE 6:36

Meditation

LORD, YOU CLAIM me as yours, just as you did on the day you stood before Pontius Pilate. In your majestic humility, you foresaw this moment of vulnerability, yet you offer all strength and life if I only pay attention to your nearness.

You knew I would often condemn you and fail to recognize and honor you in your own person, in myself, and in others. You, the fully human, complete, and divine one, faced our representative, Pilate. You, Lord, stood as a perfect mirror reflecting God's will as only silent grace could. Let the eucharistic embers teach me to dissolve with love before all that convicts me of being other than conformed to you.

Prayer

LORD OF SUBMISSION, teach me not to judge or condemn others. You undertook your passion because you loved every one of us, so how can we do less? Grant me the grace of openness to all you ask. Lord, you knew I might recognize you in the actions of the priest but fail to see you in those assembled. Help me to see you among us at every moment and to be a peacemaker.

Condemned to death, you were the jar of ointment broken out of extravagant love. I adore you in the Eucharist and beg for the grace to set aside time in my life to sit before you, letting your graces fill me, making me the vessel that is ready to be broken for others. I know that it gives you pleasure when I ask for these graces, and I pray to use them well. Amen.

Jesus Is Made to Bear His Cross

*After mocking him,
they stripped him of the robe
and put his own clothes on him.
Then they led him away to crucify him.*

MATTHEW 27:31

Meditation

YOU, LORD, LOOK up with innocent eyes. I am part of your cross. I am not heavy for you. "Let's go," you say. "I am the tool God is using, and because I love you so much I am happy to begin this walk." You were thinking of me and the happiness I would have in heaven, yet you knew I would often resist the death to myself, the journey into wholeness. With love, you anoint the dark places of my being. Your presence in the Eucharist brings light and wholeness, building on yesterday's graces.

Prayer

LORD, MY BEST FRIEND, you left a precious gift in the Eucharist. I accept the cross that comes so often in unexpected form. When I feel I can't stand the weight any longer, I pray to think about the cross I put on your shoulder. I thank God for the gift you left us. You gave us a means to become more like you.

Without the Mass and your presence among us, I would be lost. Each time we stand at the consecration and say in our hearts "this is my Body, this is my Blood," we gain a new understanding of your redemptive act that takes us deeper into the wonder of your "yes." When I receive you in the Eucharist or kneel in adoration, teach me a little more about simplicity and a love humble enough to be given away. Help me to say yes with complete trust to whatever God sends me and to look for the gift in all things. Amen.

Jesus Falls the First Time Under the Weight of His Cross

*He was despised and
rejected by others;
a man of suffering and
acquainted with infirmity.*

ISAIAH 53:3

Meditation

JESUS, YOU PLACE one foot in front of the other, a humble man going to work for those you love. No need to prod you. Nothing needed but the rightness of the moment. Once you accepted God's will, peace filled your heart. Aligned with him, you forgot the icy fingers of fear that had curled about your heart. You moved deep within your center, finding the strength for your journey.

I see you as you fall within my being. A simple trip, and the weight of your cross throws you off balance. Your agony flows into the very heart of me as you fall down. You want to reach for help but cannot. Out of love, you stifle the cry, you allow the fall, you descend…lost in love.

Prayer

LORD OF SUFFERING, you walked bleeding, feet aching, nerves in your shoulder pinched by your cross, but peace sat beside the anguish in your heart. Help us to experience that sense of rightness that brings peace when we are in alignment with the will of God. On difficult days, let me walk closely beside you.

If we look deep into your eyes, we will see the smile of recognition that says, "I know, it's all right, walk with me a bit on my way to Calvary; even if you stumble, the getting up is worth the effort. I am working for you just as you must work for those you love." I pray for the courage you modeled. I will pray for this grace when I receive you in holy Communion. Amen.

Jesus Meets His Sorrowful Mother

"[A]nd a sword will pierce your own soul too."

LUKE 2:35

Meditation

WHEN I RECEIVE holy Communion, I call up the different images of Mary that I carry deep within my soul. See the sweet mother, all silvery in love's ecstasy turned inside out. The queen of waiting waits for her son. Oh, Jesus, Mary's hands reach for you. How you long to rest your head in her hands. Her contact with you empowers. History is exploding as your eyes meet; only you two understand the shaking of the world you are now causing.

Obedience is laid down as seed for the new kingdom and planted in the ground of compassion by the fire that springs between you at this meeting. Thank you for allowing me to watch. The light that leaps between you, Lord, and your mother enfolds me in its aura of grace.

Prayer

JESUS, SON OF GOD, Son of Mary, fully human, fully divine, you left me many graces before you died. You left hope. You knew what you had to do even if it would cause pain for those close to you. It takes great courage to answer our call when perhaps those we love do not understand. Grant me the grace to go forward in answer to my particular call.

When we act in God's interest and from what is best in ourselves, we may encounter misunderstanding. People may lose confidence in us and condemn us because we do not meet their expectations. Help me to be a person Mary would be happy to claim as her own. When I must let go of someone I love, I pray to remember to turn to Mary, my model, confident that she will lead me to the Eucharist, the fruit of your passion and death. Amen.

Simon of Cyrene Helps Jesus Carry His Cross

*"No one can come to me unless
drawn by the Father who sent me;
and I will raise that person up
on the last day."*

JOHN 6:44

Meditation

MY LOVE, so weak, so tired. You are often portrayed as small or beaten down. Yet you are large enough in spirit to come to me in bread; that is how much you want to be with me, to lift me up. You, who could have called all majesty and power to your side, humbled yourself. What joy you must have felt when that awful weight was lightened, when you had a friend and were not alone.

I have forgotten to turn to you when I have been too weak and sick to stand. I have forgotten that you know what it is like to wonder how you are ever going to carry on. Oh, my Jesus, burn within me the image of Simon lifting the weight of the cross from you. Let me stand ever under that cross. Put my heart as a buffer between you and the great burden you were destined to drag so you may never feel alone.

Prayer

DEAR LORD, Man of Contradictions, sometimes we are very alone in the Church because our understanding of you differs from that of our neighbor. Differences crucified you because people were not tolerant. Please help us to accept each other, to honor and even to nurture the differences. In all that you did in your last hours, there was great symbolism. You were always trying to show us how interdependent we are.

Please help me to overcome my pride that keeps me from humbly accepting the help of other people. Please give me the wisdom to ask God for his help too. Simon was different from the crowd. He stepped forward. He followed love. Grant us the grace to love so purely and to become bread broken for each other. Amen.

Veronica Wipes the Face of Jesus

*"Blessed are the merciful,
for they will receive mercy.
Blessed are the pure in heart,
for they will see God."*

MATTHEW 5:7-8

Meditation

LORD, YOU ARE here again in such a special manner in this silent moment when all my energy is focused on your Body and Blood, soul and divinity nourishing me, helping me to be transformed into your image. Jesus, let my cells be a cloth to wipe your face and give you comfort. Imprint upon each one your likeness. Illuminate my deepest self so it will be as God willed: unique, but bearing forever the print of my eucharistic encounter with you.

You must have loved Veronica greatly to have given her such a gift: a symbolic action meant for our reflection through the ages. As you join yourself to me, press into each tissue the reminder of our meeting. Oh, Lord of my life, when the veil is pulled back, may you, most beautiful one, be all that is seen.

Prayer

LORD OF ALL BEAUTY, for each of us the Eucharist means something different. Together we make up the body of Christ; we make you present among us. Show yourself to us, Jesus, so that we may mirror you for each other. Help me not turn away from the poor and less comely and to reach out to touch you in all that I see today.

You speak in silence when you offer all of yourself in bread and wine. By meditating on your example, may I come to that purity of heart that will allow me to see the face of God. In the Eucharist, you are the great icon. Grant me the grace to spend time before you, waiting on your pleasure, adoring and loving you. Amen.

THE SEVENTH STATION

Jesus Falls the Second Time

*Let your steadfast love, O LORD,
be upon us, even as we hope in you.*

PSALM 33:22

Meditation

LORD JESUS, I am desolate. My spirits lie on the ground. Even *your* presence brings no cheer. Life seems to hold unavoidable handfuls of mud. Forgive me my lack of hope. You, O Love, are with me as host, as guest. Nothing breaks your fall. My heavy heart matches your weight as you tumble, face pressing into the bleak roughness of life. You, my God, are lying face down in the evil of this life.

While you lie so helpless and broken under the weight of the cross, the shouts and jeers of the crowd forming the walls of the cocoon in which you lie, are you thinking of all the problems in your Church today? The lack of compassion and forgiveness we show those who sin against us? As you lie on the ground, I feel the weight of your heart, heavy with anguish, holding you pinned in immobility. My love rushes to form a canopy over you. There is darkness all around us, the gray gloom of defeat in which no colored flowers can bloom or birds can sing.

Prayer

PERSEVERING LORD, *hope* could be your last name. Help me understand what it means to have this gift. You lived your life and died as you did to give us the gift of hope. You must have understood its value as no one else ever has.

Without you I would be lost. I would not be able to find my way to real freedom. No matter what pushes me down in this life, you have shown me the way up. Lord, help us to see that we are never alone. You have gone before, and you walk with us now. When I touch you in the Eucharist, eat and drink your Body and Blood, or adore you, I pray for the gifts of hope and perseverance. I pray for joy to fill my heart because you allow me to share in your suffering. Amen.

Jesus Consoles the Women of Jerusalem

*"And I tell you, everyone who
acknowledges me before others,
the Son of Man also will acknowledge
before the angels of God."*

LUKE 12:8

Meditation

LORD, HOW HUMBLY you move along the path to your death. Women push through the crowd; you see them and stop. It was often women who reached out to you during your ministry. They knew instinctively that you would heal them and that you brought a message that freed them from oppression. You reached out, knowing women needed to hear they were children of God, equal in the new kingdom.

Lord Jesus, you felt a burst of new energy when you consoled the women who met you on your route with destiny. What a relief it was for you to be taken out of yourself; you were not used to being the subject of such intense focus. Your sense of abandonment came from the prison of your suffering. It was a moment of joy to comfort those who grieved.

Prayer

COMPASSIONATE LORD, YOU give me the Eucharist. In gratitude I try to keep you in mind at all times. Help me praise and adore you by all my actions. May I never hesitate to reach out to those in need. Tender and precious is the ointment imparted to others by one who suffers. Let this precious drop of consolation that fell from your suffering being live on: the seal between your life and death, the royal seal of Jesus the Christ, the golden drop that signs all your followers, the holy oil that seeps from all true victims, the golden blaze of compassion.

I come now before you in adoration, grateful to sink in silence, speaking the language of prayer. I look at you in love, knowing that in this moment more passes between us than can ever be put into words. Amen.

Jesus Falls
the Third Time

*"We must work the works of him
who sent me while it is day;
night is coming
when no one can work."*

JOHN 9:4

Meditation

YOU, LORD OF THE UNIVERSE, a bloody mass, fell. Crushing pain pushed your body down. The ground you had slept on, the dust you had knelt on, the rocks you had told parables about—all were now enemies. The earth appeared to be caught in a scheme compounding your agony. How dark your world was as blood filled your eyes and people jeered.

I saw this happen to you when I received holy Communion. Next, I saw my own brokenness. Each pebble that hurt you was one of my sins. I felt the darkness, the bleakness, the totally turned-inside-out woundedness of my being as it joined with you. Lord Jesus, you took this on that I might be healed. I praise and adore you, Jesus, God and Man. You loved me enough to go through such treatment so that I may know everlasting joy in heaven.

Prayer

MY REDEEMER, YOU belong to us. The Creator of the universe gave you to us so that we might understand. It is only through you that we will pass to the glory of God's light. Yours is the hand that has reached out and will pull us to you when we cross to the new kingdom. I pray for self-knowledge and honesty because I want so much to see you face to face. You saw all of our sins when you lay face down on the ground.

When those around me fall through sin or from carrying heavy burdens, let me pray for them. Often we Christians are judged harshly because we are not perfect. You were telling us through your actions that you came for those who stumble, get up, and fall again but keep going. You said this in so many ways, but you mirrored it for us when you fell and got up again ready to finish the task at hand. Lord, as I adore you in the Eucharist, I reflect on the meaning of your witness to human weakness. Amen.

Jesus Is Stripped of His Garments

"In a little while the world will no longer see me, but you will see me; because I live, you also will live."

JOHN 14:19

Meditation

JESUS, IT IS too much when I try to contemplate you standing on Golgotha, being stripped of your garments. I look at you from afar and from the side. I force myself to walk around to the front and up close. I try to avoid your eyes, but they hold me fast. In that meeting there is protection for you. In our communion you are not as aware of your painful nakedness, of the harsh breaking of boundaries. You call me to stand as a shield for your vulnerability. You seek the aura of presence.

Held by those anguished eyes, I don't act out the cruelty I, too, am capable of. Asked to cover you with adoration, I forget myself and stand with you in spite of the danger. You willingly endured such treatment just to bring one person to you. You would bear humiliation just to bring one to see the truth. You would feel the tear of fabric from your wounds to move the hardest of hearts. Can we ever doubt that you are God and know us? Only our Creator could know how to get our attention.

Prayer

JESUS, SON OF GOD, my naked Lord, when I receive the host, may I recall your shivering body, naked, vulnerable, and helpless as it hung in the gallery of God's destiny. My Lord, when you come to me in the Eucharist, I experience the pure joy of celebration, the remembrance of the events of Good Friday, the celebration of all eternity. Help me build up your body on earth. Amen.

Jesus Is Nailed to the Cross

*There they crucified him,
and with him two others,
one on either side,
with Jesus between them.*

JOHN 19:18

Meditation

MY BELOVED, when the priest elevates your Body and Blood after the consecration, I see his outstretched arms as your cross. It is beautiful to see you raised up to God. By your "yes," you took all of us with you. You taught us the most when you opened your arms wide in love, collecting us in the embrace that is eternal, showing us that we most resemble you when we let go of everything. You hung there, handled by us, helpless in our hands, raised into the air of God's breath.

How intense must be the listening moment of God as you are held toward him. What a gracious God that he accepts such from his creatures. Your crucifixion lights up all of me as tissue tears, pain engulfs, and cells are moved apart. I bow in love before this act you alone were able to do in its most perfect form.

Prayer

LORD OF FORGIVENESS, you make possible life as it is contained in the Trinity. You accepted the challenge to be all that you could so I could do the same. By accepting God's will, you were God's gift to us. Help me to accept God's will in my life even when I might not understand. Help me to see you in nature, in our lovely universe, and to treat it with reverence.

Because you lived among us, I should be even more mindful of the special beauty of our land. Help me also see that you did not leave me for some far distant shore, but in your life and agony you left me three precious gifts: the way to freedom, your continued presence in the Eucharist, and the great gift of the Holy Spirit. Teach me the mystery of you, Jesus the Christ, savior and beloved of the Creator of all that is. Amen.

Jesus Dies on His Cross

*"No one has greater love than this,
to lay down one's life
for one's friends."*

JOHN 15:13

Meditation

WHEN I CLOSE my eyes to be with you after receiving the Eucharist, I'm aware of the journey again. Blood moving as a march of fire across each sin, an open wound. Your blood slowly moves over the crater, and now it is white. Crucified within me, my soul is caught up in your crucifixion. Communion is truly that: communion. The essence that springs from those wounds heal my own wounds, and you send healing again and again in the moment of holy Communion.

Prayer

JESUS, THE GREATEST LOVER, forgive me the times I don't take care of you or honor the gift that you are. Help me follow the promptings of the Holy Spirit. Your crucifixion was the ultimate exchange, the beginning of the resurrection. Your complete outpouring at the moment of death was a mouth that breathed out all the darkness of the world. Yours was an innocent heart so broken by desolation that all joy could fill the void left on earth. No one could look at your face and not see God pouring himself out totally into his world.

Such complete outpouring was the return to ultimate being, the completion of the circle, power given triumphantly away. Your death was the speaking of the glory of God into every atom and the single-minded concentration made possible by love. Your whole life was telling about God, who is love, and urging us to follow you into light and freedom. Help me wake up to that message. Amen.

Jesus Is Taken Down From the Cross and Laid in the Arms of His Mother

*[H]e has clothed me
with the garments of salvation.*

Isaiah 61:10

Meditation

JESUS, I SEE you lying across the lap of your mother. Her knees become the altar on which you complete your passion. You have brought all of us with you and laid us in her arms. In her anguish, she moves deeper inward to touch the core where you were conceived. There she finds the peace of fulfillment in her role in God's plan. She rejoices that she had a gift fit to give to almighty God. She becomes the altar from which the Eucharist springs.

Could she be more united with God than when she was kneeling at the foot of the cross, holding you and praying you were safe with God? I now pray to receive you as Mary did, in loving acceptance and unquestioning love for the action of the holy in our lives.

Prayer

MARY, MOTHER OF JESUS, the circle has been completed. In this most intimate moment we see you, the Immaculate One, holding your crucified son. Sweet Mother, teach me the wisdom of a woman's heart. You, too, are a very great gift. Let me spend time with you, attentive to your teaching.

Help me see how vulnerable Christ was. He lived in the community of others and, because of that, he knew you would be cared for. Help us dance the dance of aloneness in death while surrounded by other people. When unspeakable grief comes my way, please grant me the grace to unite my heart with you, Virgin most pure, and to hold the pain in loving union with you and in full surrender as you modeled for me. Amen.

THE FOURTEENTH STATION

Jesus Is Placed in the Tomb

" [F]or I go to prepare
a place for you."

JOHN 14:2

Meditation

WHAT IS ECSTASY but being lost in the light of full presence? The bliss that comes from an awareness of all that is utter simplicity itself. Lord, as I follow you into your tomb, light is lost. You enter that place where love is contained. God alone is love without boundary, overflowing, spilling into, filling up, pouring out all that is. We and creation become God's boundary. Perhaps the Trinity is as close to unbounded love as we can know.

Lord, you come to me within a wafer of bread, a tomb so different from the place you were laid. Both contain your being; both hold all possibilities. Your tomb and your hidden life in this sacrament require the eyes of faith. We need faith to see you living in your resurrection, and we need faith to mourn your passing from us. You were doing then what God has always done: bursting the boundaries of love. Your crucified body and soul were bread then as now. Only you could contain total awareness. You contained it all.

Prayer

JESUS, MAN AND GOD, help me to see the larger picture, to be willing to risk the unknown and work to conquer the narrowness of vision that may cause the killing of all that is good. Fear and self-centeredness create a tomb in which no new life can be found. Let your word, the membrane you left us, become our boundary.

Your time in the tomb was the prototype of your activity in our lives: filling the most ordinary of things with your presence, calling us to go beyond ourselves in love to make the joyful discovery of your tender presence in a new form. Call us out of the darkness of the tomb to look for you again and again and please, Lord, continue to surprise us. Amen.

The Resurrection of Jesus

For you shall go out in joy.

ISAIAH 55:12

Meditation

JESUS, LIVE WITH me within the world, within the Trinity. Your resurrection is ecstasy with the boundaries broken. You come in victory. You came forth from mystery to show the way to eternal life. You spoke with words and showed us by signs that you had the right to speak those words. Were that not enough, you left the Spirit to speed us on our way and the Eucharist to give us the consolation to keep going.

We should be the happiest people on earth. I am happy you show us your scars from the nails and glow with the radiance of God. The glow of your friends who carry your message touches me now with the promise of everlasting life.

Prayer

JESUS, you who are eternal, thank you for this journey. Fill me with the new life. Your resurrection is the space left by suffering in our hearts, filled now with hope. Your resurrection is your joyful surprise: the power of joy, hope, triumph, victory, and love, all contained in one gleeful happening: the ultimate "See, I told you so!"

Help me carry you out to all whom I meet today. By my patience, compassion, and joy may others' hearts swell with the goodness of life. I love you, I praise you, and I thank you for the gift you are to me in word and sacrament. My Communion thanksgiving is not very reverent: "Let's fool them all again and raise up in blazing love to live joyfully, fully, your glory shining out of me." After all, is that not what the first Easter was and is all about? Amen.